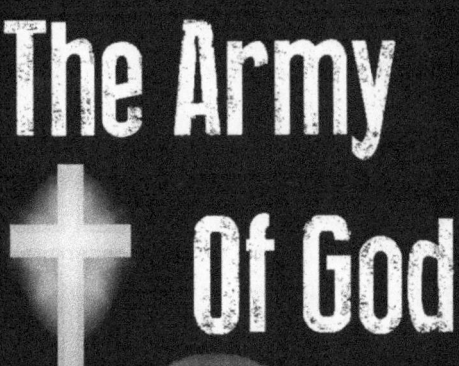

The Army Of God

Learn how to be a soldier of light battling end time darkness.

DR. DONALD BELL
MAJOR USMC | RET.

The Army of God
Learn how to be a soldier of light battling end-of-this-age darkness.
August 2018
Copyright © Dr. Donald Bell

All rights reserved. Printed in the United States of America. No part of this publication may be reproduced, stored in a retrieval system, or transmitted, in any form or by any means electronic, mechanical, photocopying, recording, or otherwise, without the prior written permission of the author.

Scripture taken from the Holy Bible, English Standard Version (ESV) ®. Copyright © 2001 by Crossway, a publishing ministry of Good Publishers. Used by permission. All rights reserved.

ISBN 978-1-943412-09-9

Published by -
Wilderness Voice Publishing, LLC
Canon City, Colorado USA
www.wvpbooks.com

"A voice crying in the wilderness –
proclaiming the good news of the coming Kingdom!"

Contents

Introduction	5
A Call to the Frontlines *"Volunteers Only"*	6
A Spiritual War	7
A Church Problem *So Few Warriors in Leadership*	8
Leadership in the Army of God	9
Warriors on the Battlefield of Life	13
What Our Mission "IS NOT"	14
Our Authority as Soldiers in the Army of God	16
Comradeship	18
A Very Powerful Bonding Among His Soldiers	17
Discipline in the Army of God	20
Christian Warriors: We are called to "FAST"	21
True Christianity *A Life of Self-Sacrifice*	25
Combating Confusion	27
Imprisonment *A Favorite Tactic of the Enemy*	28
Growing Stronger	30
Glorious Benefits of Tribulation	31
Christian Warriors - "No Compromise" *Endure Persecution*	31
Evil Disguised as Decency	33
Our Lord Tarries - Why?	33
Additional Resources	36

INTRODUCTION

This is not a message of eternal salvation nor is it intended for those Christians who are content with their current status. This message is intended for those Christians who possess a "warrior spirit" deep inside and are searching for their individual position within the Army of God. Men and women who really want to stand strong for our Lord in the face of a world that is becoming increasingly darker year after year. A people who will not shy away from being counted among those in His Army who will accept these words of Jesus:

"If the world hates you, know that it has hated me before it hated you. If you were of the world, the world would love you as its own; but because you are not of the world, but I chose you out of the world, therefore the world hates you. Remember the word that I said to you: 'A servant is not greater than his master.' If they persecuted me, they will also persecute you" (John 15:18-20).

The opportunity to become that Champion that God is looking for is available to all, but history and experience shows that very few have the desire to step into this arena.

But, for those who want to make a deep impact for the Kingdom of God in their lifetime, we are on the verge of time that will require a great need for "champion" style leaders in the Body of Christ.

I am hopeful that this message will help inspire and give some understanding to those whose desire it is to: "love our LORD with all of the "heart", "soul", "mind" and "strength".

I emphasize "strength" because of the huge sacrifice that "champions" must undergo to "finish that race" which GOD calls them to.

A CALL TO THE FRONTLINES – "VOLUNTEERS ONLY"

Now the army of the Lord is composed only of "volunteers." Jesus Christ, our Commander-in-Chief does not draft His soldiers, but He opens His arms and welcomes all those who volunteer. He does not employ emotional gimmickry, but simply speaks out of love and calls each of us to join Him on the battlefield.

Although he calls us to join Him in His battle against the forces of evil, He leaves us free to join the enemy against him if we so will.

He makes no promises that we will become rich or not experience pain in this life.

The belief that His army will be entirely free from injuries, strife, pain, and poverty is an invention of the "health and wealth" gospel that is not found in Scripture or in the Christian experience.

As volunteer soldiers in His army, like our Lord, we will grieve and bleed and perhaps lose our lives for our brothers and sisters who are not yet freed from the enemy. However, we are promised the ultimate victory and if we fight, His pleasure will rest upon us.

Our Lord does not encourage us to join Him simply because we want to be on the winning team, but He wants us to join because we believe in the righteousness of His cause.

Volunteers must also understand that we will die in our faith, while not really receiving all of God's promises in this life. This is not an armchair war and it will be very difficult for many in our generation to make the adjustment from being spectators to becoming active participants. We all need to understand that the way to eternal life with Christ involves the way of the Cross. And the way of the Cross means there is a great battle to be fought.

A SPIRITUAL WAR

First, we must recognize that we are up against an enemy who is incredibly powerful; one whom the great majority of the world's population embraces. Since the days of mankind's Fall in the Garden of Eden, there has been ongoing warfare against the devil and all his evil hosts on earth as well as in heaven.

Over and over, the Scriptures reveal that there is a violent, ongoing war occurring in the spiritual realm in which the people of GOD on earth must actively participate. The New Testament Christian, like the Old Testament Israelite, continues to be engaged in a battle, and it is a battle: *"Not directed against flesh and blood, but against the rulers, against the authorities, against the powers of this dark world, and against the spiritual forces of evil in the heavenly realms"* (Ephesians 6:12).

In the dark times that are rapidly approaching, it will be very costly not to be in our assigned place in the Lord's kingdom.

Although the days are becoming darker & darker, those who are responding to "His Calling" will experience ever-increasing peace, joy, and fulfillment in what we are called to do.

Both the light and the darkness are coming to full maturity in these times and thus, evil is also mobilizing for the battle against the forces of light.

It is time for each one of us to find our place in the Army of the Lord. When we are in our assigned place, we will know it. If we are questioning whether we are in the right place or not, we can be pretty sure we are not.

Ask the Lord for your assigned place in His army. Here is the way – you must become a living sacrifice unto God:

"I appeal to you therefore, brothers, by the mercies of God, to present your bodies as a living sacrifice, holy and acceptable to God, which is your spiritual worship. Do not be conformed to this world, but be transformed by the renewal of your mind, that by testing you may discern what is the will of God, what is good and acceptable and perfect" (Romans 12:1-2).

A CHURCH PROBLEM
SO FEW WARRIORS IN LEADERSHIP

Now the modern-day evangelical church acknowledges an ongoing spiritual warfare but in reality, it functions as if it is only passively involved.

The traditional church tends to busy itself with the more internal and visible aspects of local church life and thus, many Christians come to believe that there is nothing more to do except to "attend Sunday services and occasionally participate in weekly bible studies".

This appears to encompass the complete Christian life. Thus, most Christians are living as if there is no on-going spiritual warfare.

Yet, if that is how one is to live out the Christian life, why is the church so impotent in this country? Why is darkness so rapidly increasing in America?

Why are there so many divorce, adultery, pornography, and abortions within the evangelical church?

It's like America and much of the church are on a downhill roller-coaster ride going faster and faster into a deepening darkness. Messages that are non-offensive are the primary teachings from the pulpit.

There is a growing frustration, especially among men, concerning the ministry of the traditional church within the

Christian life. Recent polls taken by George Barna reveal that nearly 50% of "born again" men are not regular attendees of Sunday church services. Why?

I believe that deep inside numerous non-church Christians, is a warrior spirit that desires to stand for the kingdom of God against the dark enemies on the battlefield of life.

And the traditional church services popular "entertainment" and "easy believism" and "worldly prosperity" messages cannot feed that "warrior spirit". Numerous "hungry men" disrespect pastors as superficial "wimps" or "goody goodies" with whom they cannot identify.

These are men who hunger for strong, Christian leadership to rise up and call them together into the Lord's Army.

LEADERSHIP IN THE ARMY OF GOD

God's leadership calling for this generation must understand, and internalize the following truth if they intend to prevail in their mission:

> The great warriors of the Bible all experienced challenging tribulations in life as they were being prepared in order that they could be brought into the purposes of God.
>
> Between those places where we receive the promise and the fulfillment of the promise, there will be a wilderness experience that is the exact opposite of what has been promised.
>
> The purpose of the wilderness journey is to conform us to the image of Jesus Christ and to bring us to a place of maturity where He can trust us with more authority.

Some Biblical examples of Warriors standing for the Kingdom of God:

God's Warriors	vs.	Satan's Warriors
David	vs.	Goliath
Moses	vs.	Pharaoh
Elijah	vs.	Ahab, Jezebel, Baal Prophets
Joseph	vs.	10 Brothers & Potiphar's Wife
Gideon & 300	vs.	15,000 Midianite Army
Jesus & Disciples	vs.	Worldly Religious Leaders
Christian Martyrs	vs.	Roman Empire
Christian Martyrs	vs.	Roman Catholicism
Christian Martyrs	vs.	Stalin, Hitler, Mao Zedong
Christian Martyrs	vs.	Muslim Armies
Today's Christians	vs.	Worldly Governments
Today's Christians	vs.	Invasion of Church Liberalism
Today's Christians	vs.	New Age Religions

For 6,000 Years:

Kingdom of God	vs.	Kingdom of the World

These events certainly stand out, but we need to remember that life is a battlefield where God's people are confronted again and again by Satan's chosen vessels.

The whole history of the church is the arena of God versus Satan in "Trials by Ordeal." It hasn't changed; but it is about to get more challenging than ever before.

Satan's champions will always visibly appear to be greater and more powerful than God's champions.

Yet, warrior-spirited Christians standing uncompromisingly for our Lord will always prevail in the strength of the Lord.

Remember, there is no victory without a battle. Christian leaders must see every test as a great opportunity and no matter how dark it seems to get, the light will surely dawn, just as the sun comes up in the morning.

Some hard truths that Leadership must prepare for:
1. This world is in iniquity and will fight to the last against Jesus Christ and His Kingdom on this earth.
2. The heavenly Kingdom of God will come only after worldwide wars evolving in the persecution of the church that will separate the true Christians from the false.
3. There is an apostate part of the church that will compromise and align itself with the world leading to betrayal of other Christians.
4. It is through times of tribulation that true righteousness is clearly manifested.

Good versus Great Leadership

There are many "good" leaders in the Church. Good leaders get things done in normal times and we can generally get by with "good" leaders.

But, we are no longer living in normal times and we need "great" leaders who will display both courage and wisdom in the face of unprecedented challenges. We need "good" leaders, but we are desperate for "great" leaders.

A Military Perspective of a Great Leader

A leader does not abide in his tent while his men bleed and die upon the field. A leader does not dine while his men go hungry, nor sleep when they stand at watch upon the wall. A leader does not command his men's loyalty through fear, nor purchase it with gold; he earns their love by the sweat of his own back and the pains he endures for their sake. That which comprises the harshest burden, a leader lifts first and sets down last. A leader does not require service of those he leads but provides it to them. He serves them, not they him.

Does this remind you of the greatest Leader that ever walked on the earth?

Consider this: Many may have been called to this leadership role, yet they did not forsake their lives and thus, did not achieve their full calling. They certainly are among the saints of God, but they did not attain to the leadership role that God had prepared them for.

- Knighthood of Christian Warriors -

God's potential leaders in His army must first prevail with the Lord Himself.

These chosen leaders can prevail with God only as they are brought to their knees in submission before Him on a day-by-day basis. These are the warrior-spirited Christians.

It is God, not us, who is the real conqueror of Satan, but many of us will be eternally honored as a type of overcoming soldier that our Commander-in-Chief is searching for among His people.

Leaders of soldiers in the Army of God in these last days must be totally committed to walk the pathway that the Lord, our Commander-in-Chief, has laid before them.

Therefore, it is important to internalize our understanding of the mission to which He has called us.

This mission exists in the passion of each leader's heart and direction becomes clearer as it is written down and internalized each day.

> **Example of an Individual's Mission Statement**
> *To visibly magnify the glorious light of Jesus Christ by living out the Spirit of the Gospel in my life in such a way that it will positively affect others in the Army of God for the strengthening and expanding of our Lord's Kingdom amidst the troubling days which are shortly before us.*

My Christian friends, we can be part of greatest force for good in this world if we are willing to change and become the soldiers we are called to be. It does not matter how many mistakes we have made, or how many years we have wasted. It does not matter how old or how young we are – we can still be a part of His army.

If we will make all of our major decisions based upon seeking the Kingdom of God and His righteousness first, then He promises that everything we need will be provided for us.

Remember this - we can be in the wrong place and still have a great job and be financially well off, but inside we will feel empty and without peace when we are alone.

WARRIORS ON THE BATTLEFIELD OF LIFE

God's army may not be large, but there has never been one more powerful. They refuse to retreat before the enemies of the Cross and their faithfulness that may lead to death is far more powerful than death itself. Soldiers in the army of God are not fearful of dying because they have already died to the things of this world and they live to do all things for the sake of the gospel. Mighty warriors of God would never run from the sound of a battle for they know that there cannot be a victory without a battle.

"For the word of the cross is foolishness to those who are perishing, but to us who are being saved it is the power of God" (1 Corinthians 1:18).

Soldiers in His army must take up the Cross daily, not occasionally.

Our life focus is to seek the will of the Lord, not our own will. However, those in the army of God will experience a wilderness journey in this life.

We must learn to endure the hard times in order to get to the land flowing with milk and honey.

However, we will also experience wonderful things in the wilderness for that is also the dwelling place of God in the midst of His people.

A Sound principle: Anything that happens too fast or too easily is usually insignificant for spiritual development.

Intense boot camp-like training will definitely develop mighty warrior-spirited witness for Christ in His army.

Now, when I'm speaking of warfare which the Army of God is called to confront in this world, I want to clarify:

WHAT OUR MISSION "IS NOT"

Soldiers in the army of God need to understand that we are not forces of revolution attempting to establish a righteous government in this present world. This world is not our home; until it is finally liberated, it belongs to the enemy. In fact, soldiers in God's army are despised by the world.

"Do not love the world or the things in the world. If anyone loves the world, the love of the Father is not in him. For all that is in the world— the desires of the flesh and the desires of the eyes and pride in possessions—is not from the Father but is from the world. And the world is passing away along with its desires, but whoever does the will of God abides forever" (1 John 2:15-17).

Our army is probably better characterized as guerillas behind enemy lines with a mission to proclaim the true gospel message of Jesus Christ, as the Son of God, to those currently in the world.

As soldiers in this army, we will be continually ridiculed, scorned, and persecuted; yet the greater the persecution, the more powerful the gospel message becomes as the evilness of the world becomes more and more visible to the masses when they witness the tremendous hatred toward those who possess a heart of love.

Our assigned mission is to lead those held in captivity by the world:

- Out of the darkness of this world & into the light of the Lord's kingdom.
- From the deception of this world unto the truth found in the Lord's kingdom.
- From the evilness of this world into the righteousness of the Lord's kingdom.
- From eternal damnation and misery into eternal life and joy in the Lord's kingdom.

We thought this was our mission in Vietnam – to free the South Vietnamese from the bondage of communism – but America, who is a worldly kingdom, turned their back on those who were fighting to free others. Many of the South Vietnamese, who had supported and trusted America, were subsequently tortured, raped, and murdered when our country abandoned them and allowed the communists to sweep down from the north and take over. Our government betrayed the South Vietnamese who had placed their trust in us.

But the kingdom of God, led by our Lord will never betray His soldiers fighting to free others.

Jesus Christ will continually encourage and strengthen us to "make war, because we love."

OUR AUTHORITY AS SOLDIERS IN THE ARMY OF GOD

Accepting responsibility is the nature of God's will. Some may think it unfair that others would be affected by our obedience or disobedience.

Consider the consequences of Adam's disobedience. Adam did not ask to be in a position where his actions would affect billions of his offspring. However, he was given authority over the earth and with authority comes responsibility.

The clear teaching throughout Scripture is that what we do affects others. The greater the authority, the greater the impact will be, for good or bad.

We have not been called just to be saved and go to heaven, but rather we have a purpose to fulfill.

Like it or not, we are called to be "soldiers in the army of God." There is a significant difference between soldiers of the world & soldiers in God's army:

Soldiers of the world may die carrying out a mission to kill the enemy and take prisoners captive.

Soldiers in the kingdom of God may die carrying out a mission to love the enemy and release prisoners from spiritual captivity. The weapons that we fight with are "spiritual" not "carnal."

All Christian soldiers in the Army of God do lose some battles now and then, but they continue to be strengthened by their experiences and do not succumb to self-pity.

If we embrace the Cross we no longer have the right to go our own way.

We have a calling, a mission. While being a soldier in God's army is a responsibility, it is also an opportunity.

You could be used to set many free from captivity.

Perhaps, you are not called to the frontlines of the battlefield, but according to biblical standards, those called to support soldiers on the frontlines will also receive their reward similar to those who are called to the front.

The authority that Satan is currently exercising over the earth is a usurped authority.

It is not the Lord's authority that he has usurped, but man's. Dominion over the earth was given to man.

The Lord respects this, which is why Jesus had to become a man to reclaim that authority as the Son of Man.

And just as Satan uses people to do his will, the Lord likewise exercises his authority through His people.

The earth was given to man to rule and the Lord will rule over it through man.

Now why did the Lord not take His authority over the earth immediately after He was resurrected?

Because He knows that the ongoing battle between good and evil trains His soldiers to use His authority.

We are called to rule with Him in the age to come, and the Lord is seeking those who will mature in Him and walk in His authority.

COMRADESHIP

"I do not ask for these only, but also for those who will believe in me through their word, that they may all be one, just as you, Father, are in me, and I in you, that they also may be in us, so that the world may believe that you have sent me" (John 17:20-21).

Being in the Lord's army is much more than just fighting battles. It also is about uniting in community with Him – to be built into a spiritual family that will spend eternity together.

Comradeship in combat is one of the deepest and unique bonds one can experience. Those who have experienced combat know that when the bullets start flying, you are not fighting for your country as much as for the life of the soldier next to you.

Those who go through the fire together develop a unique heart bonding with one another. This is why so many combat veterans who return home want to turn around and go back and be with their comrades once again.

If you ask someone who was in the military what they miss the most, you will seldom hear that it was the war or the country's mission. Rather it is the men in their unit who stood together during very challenging times.

This same principle is true in the army of God. This strong fellowship is also meant to be among those in the army of God – a bonding so close that those who are part of it cannot be separated.

This was certainly the characteristic of those who strongly supported David and became known as "mighty men of Israel." They could not be defeated.

Also, the Lord's twelve disciples changed the world more than any worldly conqueror.

However, the greatest and most glorious difference between soldiers in the army of God and those in the world is that every "private" in God's army has access to a personal relationship with the Commander-in-Chief.

In fact, Jesus will share His plans with the lowliest warrior who desires to know His ways.

The "private" can come boldly into the throne room at any time and be most welcome.

"O righteous Father, even though the world does not know you, I know you, and these know that you have sent me. I made known to them your name, and I will continue to make it known, that the love with which you have loved me may be in them, and I in them" (John 17:25-26).

A VERY POWERFUL BONDING AMONG HIS SOLDIERS

"Truly, I say to you, whatever you bind on earth shall be bound in heaven, and whatever you loose on earth shall be loosed in heaven. Again I say to you, if two of you agree on earth about anything they ask, it will be done for them by my Father in heaven. For where two or three are gathered in my name, there am I among them" Matthew 18:18-20

Now what does it really mean for 2 or 3 to come together? It means to be "bonded" together.

That is, to bond at the depth that the Lord is seeking, we must start with 2 or 3. Marine units in the military also use this principle.

These units are built on 4-man fire-teams. Three of these teams make up a squad and three squads make up a platoon, and then it grows through the organization of companies, battalions, regiments, and divisions.

Yet the basic foundational unit of the Corps is these four-man fire-teams. In a combat firefight, these fire-teams are more committed to each other than the larger unit. They have bonded together in like-mindedness.

Jesus' greatest works and deepest teachings were given to small groups. He did not walk on the water in front of everyone. Could it be that the Lord prefers doing His greatest miracles with the fewest witnesses? The Lord had a ministry to the multitudes but He gave far more attention to His closest disciples.

With the 12 He went much deeper and invested more time. Then with the three (Peter, James, & John), He shared everything.

Balanced ministries need to have relationships on all three levels.

The temple was also divided into three sections: The Outer Court for the multitude; the Holy Place for a few ministers; and then the Holy of Holies where only one could go.

DISCIPLINE IN THE ARMY OF GOD

"'My son, do not regard lightly the discipline of the Lord, nor be weary when reproved by him. For the Lord disciplines the one he loves, and chastises every son whom he receives.' It is for discipline that you have to endure. God is treating you as sons. For what son is there whom his father does not discipline? If you are left without discipline, in which all have participated, then you are illegitimate children and not sons" (Hebrews 12:5-8).

Now the Lord may allow hard times to strike His sons and daughters because He loves them so much. We must understand that the hard trials in this life come upon God's people because He loves them, not because He is punishing them. It is for discipline.

Those who have entered military service are thankful for the toughest drill sergeants.

Though we may hate them in boot camp, once in combat we quickly realize those sergeants cared enough to prepare us for the challenges that we face.

So, we must embrace the Lord's tough training of His army. If we pander to other people's weaknesses, we only feed the weakness that keeps them in bondage. For example: Like people admiring Bruce Jenner for his transvestite, effeminate lifestyle – those who praise him throw him deeper and darker into bondage.

Those who would witness to Bruce that what he has done is sinful are those who truly love him as they try to break the bondage that has handcuffed him.

CHRISTIAN WARRIORS
WE ARE CALLED TO "FAST"

As we approach the end of this age, we need to rediscover one of the lost secrets of the early church; that is, the power that is released through the biblical practice of "fasting unto God." Now it is true that there are many things besides food that may hinder our communion with God and it is also true that we need to practice self-denial. However, the biblical truth still remains that "to fast" means primarily "not to eat." The Greek word for "fast" is "nesteuo" which means "not to eat." Fasting has always been an important discipline throughout the Word of God.

It has been said that the quickest way to a man's heart is through his stomach. Though God has planted instinctive appetites within our bodies for our ongoing well-being, we are required to keep our physical bodies subservient to our spirit. The body is to be our servant, not our master. For each believer, there is a fine line between satisfying the normal desires of the body from a fleshly craving that stifles our inner spirit. In our western culture, food is an ever-present temptation to which we constantly yield and to which we overindulge.

So many Christians are oblivious of their bondage to food and to the fact that there is a leakage of spiritual power in their lives. What they believe is a natural and healthy appetite is really a lust that enslaves them to their physical bodies. The truth that Christian discipleship involves self-discipline in this realm has been put out of their minds.

PURPOSES FOR FASTING

1. SEEKING PERSONAL HOLINESS
> *"Humble yourselves, therefore, under the mighty hand of God so that at the proper time he may exalt you"* (1 Peter 5:6).

Humility is foundational for true holiness. Fasting is a corrective to a prideful heart. Pride and a too-full stomach are old bedfellows. Because of our natural tendency toward self-pride, we need to, like King David, humble ourselves with fasting from time to time.

Fasting is equated with "humility." Setting aside time when you would rather watch television = humility. Putting the Lord before any of your bodily desires = humility. Humility is NOT a weakness! Just the opposite: It takes great strength to pick up your cross and follow the Lord.

God foresaw that these same circumstances of pride and fullness of stomach would be one of Israel's pitfalls when they entered the Promised Land. Moses reminded them prior to entering the land:

> *"And you shall remember the whole way that the Lord your God has led you these forty years in the wilderness, that he might humble you, testing you to know what was in your heart, whether you would keep his commandments or not. And he humbled you and let you hunger and fed you with manna, which you did not know, nor did your fathers know, that he might make you know that man does not live by bread alone, but man lives by every word that comes from the mouth of the Lord"* (Deuteronomy 8:2-3).

There is a natural sequence as we move from self-humbling to prayerfully mourning for the sins of others. The eyes of the Lord continually search the earth for the Ezras who will weep and pray for the sins of a faithless people; or for the Nehemiahs who weep and mourn, fast and pray over the broken nation of America.

2. FASTING TO BE HEARD BY GOD

Fasting is connected with the desire to:

> ➤ Seek God with all your heart – then Draw near to Him – then Prevail with Him in prayer

When a person is willing to set aside the legitimate appetites of his body to concentrate on the work of praying, he is demonstrating that he means business. That he is seeking with all his heart and will not let go until he gets answers from God. Fasting confirms one's resolution to sacrifice anything to attain what we seek from the Kingdom of God.

Of course, we must not think of fasting as a hunger strike to force God's hand and get our own way. Prayer is much more complex than asking a loving Father to supply His child's needs. Prayer is warfare! Prayer is wrestling! There are opposing forces.

> ➤ *"For we do not wrestle against flesh and blood, but against the rulers, against the authorities, against the cosmic powers over this present darkness, against the spiritual forces of evil in the heavenly places"* (Ephesians 6:12).

Fasting is calculated to bring a sense of urgency into our praying. It is our expression of earnestness for seeking God's appointed way. He is using the means that God has chosen to make his voice to be heard in the heavens. Prayer with fasting is giving heaven notice that we are truly in earnest.

3. FASTING TO FREE THE CAPTIVES

> ➤ *"Is not this the fast that I choose: to loose the bonds of wickedness, to undo the straps of the yoke, to let the oppressed go free, and to break every yoke?"* (Isaiah 58:6).

The nature of "fasting" is not to bring man into bondage, but to loose them from it. So many peoples among mankind are bound with invisible shackles of the enemy. A large and continually growing proportion of our generation is hopelessly bound by alcohol, drugs, gambling, pornography, and illicit sexual desires.

Many professing Christians are also bound by anger, fear, jealousy, resentment and such things that continually bind them from truly walking with Christ. But how to get free? They may try hard to pray, to believe, to claim, - yet they remain bound.

Understandably, we need to seek the Lord's anointing for such a ministry of deliverance which He promises to His faithful disciples. **Discipleship fasting is a powerful weapon appointed by God, to break the enemy's hold over people. A "fast" undertaken at God's direction will strengthen an intercessory prayer warrior to maintain pressure on the enemy until he is compelled to loosen his grip on the captive(s).** Then "fasting" will give authority, when God's moment comes, to speak the commanding word that generates the release from bondage.

Our Lord wants us to know His own deep compassion for these tormented souls and He has given us the authority to deliver them which is part of the "great commission" (Mark 16:17).

4. FASTING FOR REVELATION

> *"I, Daniel...turned my face to the Lord God, seeking Him by prayer and supplications with fasting...Gabriel...said to me, O Daniel, I have now come out to give you wisdom and understanding"* (Daniel 9:2,3,21,22).

There should be no doubt that there is a very close connection between the practice of "fasting" and receiving spiritual revelation.

It has been said that in the last days:

"And in the last days it shall be, God declares, that I will pour out my Spirit on all flesh, and your sons and your daughters shall prophesy, and your young men shall see visions, and your old men shall dream dreams" (Acts 2:17).

Surely this will apply to many who seek God with "fasting." However, these are not the only revelations that our Lord provides His seeking people – we may get it as He brings fresh light through His holy word or by some other means such as bringing a prophetic word from another Christian.

But the need for these challenging times is the "spirit of wisdom and revelation" which is given to those who continually seek God with "prayer and fasting." Certainly, the promise given long ago to those who keep God's chosen fast is still true:

> *"Then shall your light rise in the darkness and your gloom be as the noonday. And the Lord will guide you continually and satisfy your desire in scorched places and make your bones strong; and you shall be like a watered garden, like a spring of water, whose waters do not fail"* (Isaiah 58:10-11)

For the Christian to be a warrior in the Army of Christ, he must take control over his body through self-discipline. He cannot allow his body to dictate his direction in life.

TRUE CHRISTIANITY
A LIFE OF SELF-SACRIFICE

"Share in suffering as a good soldier of Christ Jesus. No soldier gets entangled in civilian pursuits, since his aim is to please the one who enlisted him" (2 Timothy 2:3-4).

So many American churches emphasize prosperity, easy believism, doctrines that project a joyful, lazy lifestyle if you only give your life over to Christ.

On the contrary true soldiers who enlist in the U.S. Army know they are making a commitment to go into harm's way for a righteous cause and perhaps pay the ultimate price for this cause.

Soldiers in the army of God go even further by resolving to die to this world and live for the sake of the gospel.

If we die to this world, then there is nothing this world can do to us.

One who is dead does not fear rejection or failure. Being a soldier of the Cross is both the hardest and the easiest life we could live.

It is hard because resisting our selfish fleshly nature is very difficult.

At the same time, it is easy because living by the new nature of Christ is the most wonderful life we could live.

So many Christians in the American churches are looking for what God can do for them in this world, but a warrior in the army of God does not enlist for the rewards but does it to fight for righteousness. We were bought with the ultimate price – God's own life. The rewards are far greater than any that we could receive in the world.

Those who suffer persecution for His Name are mightily worthy of His kingdom.

We must understand that God wants us to be engaged on the battlefield that lies in the midst of this world.

We may certainly suffer persecution from the worldly darkness, but when that happens, remember that God considers those who do suffer persecution as mightily worthy of His kingdom.

"Pride" causes us to do almost anything to avoid shame, but that should be a sure sign that we are not yet dead to this world and alive to Christ.

Note how the apostles responded with rejoicing after the Sanhedrin had them flogged.

"Then they left the presence of the council, rejoicing that they were counted worthy to suffer dishonor for the name" (Acts 5:41).

It is a great honor in this life to suffer for the name of the Lord. We are not to seek persecution unnecessarily, but rather let it be the result of living in the light and proclaiming the truth. When persecution comes, we should not only embrace it, but rejoice in it as did the apostles.

When we lay down our lives, we truly find them. This is a comfort and peace far beyond what the world can give us.

This doesn't mean we will be free of life problems, but as we fight the spiritual battle we are assured of victory.

Therefore, endure life's problems knowing that things will work out for the good.

"We know that we are from God, and the whole world lies in the power of the evil one" (1 John 5:19). We are told the whole world lies under the power of the evil one.

This means that when we are born-again, we are now behind enemy lines and the enemy is all around as we witness in today's American culture.

COMBATING CONFUSION

Confusion is one of the most dominating factors in combat that results in defeat.

Good leadership will step up and take the initiative to be decisive in the midst of confusion.

Because confusion and uncertainty is so commonplace in the world, those with confidence in the direction they are going will inspire others.

"Courage" is a necessary element to achieve victory and imparting courage to others is basic to leadership.

Those who will follow spiritual leaders must believe in our calling from God and our ability to accomplish God's purposes.

In John 10, we are told that His sheep know His voice and follow him.

However, it goes not say that His lambs know His voice.

Lambs follow other sheep until they mature and come to know the Shepherd's voice for themselves.

Our goal as leaders is not to teach people to obey us, but rather to hear the Lord for themselves and respond to His will decisively. The Lord is not a "micromanager."

He did not lead His apostles around by the hand, but rather He sent them out.

They made their decisions and if correction was needed He would correct them perhaps through a dream or revelation.

IMPRISONMENT
A FAVORITE TACTIC OF THE ENEMY

One may wonder why imprisonment of many of God's people is employed by the enemy instead of simply executing them.

Imprisonment allows time for the enemy to break down the spirit of people for the purpose of allowing them to voluntarily turn away from the Lord and render allegiance to world authorities.

Though deep in their heart they may still believe in the Lord, some will give up. Ultimately, their life in this world will mean more to them than their faith in Christ.

Satan rejoices when men visibly turn away from Almighty God and render allegiance to him, even if it is not from a pure heart. Turning people to him is more important than murdering them, for it means he has defeated what is most important to God - the steadfast faithfulness of His people.

The one who has turned away from the Lord undoubtedly will be praised before the world as a newly enlightened hero. This will be a shameful experience.

Remain steadfast! Our Lord will provide a hiding place for us when the time of persecution arrives. Where is that hiding place?

- ➢ For the prophet Daniel, it was both in a king's palace and in a lion's den.
- ➢ For Shadrach, Meshach, and Abednego, it was in a fiery furnace.
- ➢ For Joseph, it was in an Egyptian prison.
- ➢ For David, it was in a cave out in the wilderness.
- ➢ For the apostle Paul, it was in prison or shipwrecked in the Mediterranean.
- ➢ For the spies sent by Joshua, it was in a harlot's house in Jericho.
- ➢ For Corrie Ten Boom, it was in a flea-infested barracks in a Nazi concentration camp.

They were all right where God wanted them and not a hair on their head perished. So, our hiding place is wherever the center of the Lord's will is for us.

The only thing we should fear is being out of God's will.

Trust in the Lord for our individual hiding places for they will probably be different for every believer in the End Times.

Meanwhile stand in the gap and prepare our brothers and sisters for the coming hour of trial.

Although Christians will be physically overcome during this horrendous period of time; they are the ones who are victorious in this war.

They have become outcasts from society, mocked at by former neighbors, family members, and friends, imprisoned and killed.

This is the Body of Christ having a similar experience that their Lord Jesus Christ endured 2,000 years earlier.

They are now glorious participants in His great victory. In the crucial test of faith, they have chosen to relinquish their lives rather than their faith in their God. This is true victory.

"Christian warriors, we are called to fight, not run from the battle."

GROWING STRONGER

Our salvation was freely given to us, but it was not without cost. It was bought at a cost greater than all the world's treasures – by the blood of the Son of God. He purchased us by His sacrifice.

We are not our own but belong to Him who alone could pay this price. We dishonor what deserves the greatest honor when we daily behave as if our salvation was cheap.

It was freely given to us as a gift of great value and we should treat it as such. Also, while we are freely given salvation, the Scriptures are clear that our eternal position and rewards are earned in this life.

If we seek Him, we will find Him.

If we draw near to Him, He promises to draw near to us.

How close to Him do you want to be?

We need to develop our mission for drawing closer and closer to Him (Prayer/Fasting/Worship)

Motivated peoples are easily led, but a higher form of leadership is to inspire "dry bones." (Ezekiel 37).

Where is the leadership that can gather the discouraged and disconnected, mobilizing them with a vision and purpose?

A rising prophetic ministry is an ability to see others as they are called to be. No Christian is called to be dry—we need to be a source of living water for those who are thirsty.

The work of transformation may begin with teaching, but it must be followed with equipping and deploying.

Training people is more than teaching them what to do; it is showing them how to do it and then coaching them as they try.

GLORIOUS BENEFITS OF TRIBULATION

Those in the Army of God need to understand that the end-time tribulation is like birth pangs that bring something positive into the world.

The tribulation will give birth to the second coming of Jesus, and there can be no birth without pain.

Tribulation is not something for believers to enjoy; however, it is not something for us to run from either.

A wonderful purpose for tribulation is to present an opportunity for lost people to come to repentance, for it is a period of time that will bring in the "final harvest."

For when God's judgments fall on the world, many will turn to righteousness.

"My soul yearns for you in the night; my spirit within me earnestly seeks you. For when your judgments are in the earth, the inhabitants of the world learn righteousness" (Isaiah 26:9).

Thus, God's warrior-spirited Army needs to embrace this opportunity to minister in the midst of tribulation, for it is the most important mission that we could possibly be assigned.

CHRISTIAN WARRIORS
"NO COMPROMISE" ENDURE PERSECUTION

In the coming days, true believers in Jesus Christ will be challenged from every direction. Every believer who commits to an all-out relationship with our Lord will come under governmental oppression, various afflictions, and persecution.

We may initially struggle in our trials because discipline and suffering is foreign to us, but as we continue to endure, we will recognize how meaningful the discipline of the Lord really is.

Our hearts will continually grow deeper in our love and commitment to Him.

At times it may seem unbearable when some friends and even family members become spiteful toward us.

Yet, enduring the scorn and persecution from the world joins us in a partnership with Christ as we share in His sufferings in this life.

Suffering with Christ produces a strong heart bond in our relationship with Him and with one another as we follow Him down the same path that He walked.

In order to better comprehend this, consider the following: Marines in combat who experience really tough trials together eventually grow in strength and closeness with one another.

Marines will put their own lives on the line for their fellow Marines. Yet a heart that experiences the hardships that Christ also experienced produces a much greater bond than what Marines share with each other.

For a deep spiritual love for one another begins to grow which will throw off all the cares of this world and focus only upon the Kingdom of God in this world.

Listen to Paul speaking to his disciple, Timothy:

"Share in suffering as a good soldier of Christ Jesus. No soldier gets entangled in civilian pursuits, since his aim is to please the one who enlisted him" (2 Timothy 2:3-4).

'Endure suffering son! You are a soldier in the Lord's army. You have been trained to undergo hardship on the spiritual battlefield."

EVIL DISGUISED AS DECENCY

Satan will undoubtedly attack many with, "this is too hard.... it's not fair.... God has forsaken me."

Be aware that when these thoughts begin to surface that you are a soldier in the Army of God under attack. Stand fast.

Evil disguised as decency, together with a lukewarm Christian community, may be strong weapons the enemy will use against you. They will attack your faith and attempt to get you to make compromises so that life won't be so hard.

This will be tough when loved ones embrace you and try to get you to compromise your faith just a little bit by saying, "God will understand."

Fight this! Your steadfastness is of tremendous importance to both you and your loved ones who are considering small compromises.

OUR LORD TARRIES — WHY?

Day and night, God's intercessors have cried out to the Lord that His kingdom will come, and righteous judgment will occur on the earth. Yet our Lord tarries.

Though He is at work every moment of every day, it is not always as we wish or in ways that are visible to us. He is on the throne of justice; so, we may wonder just how long justice can be postponed.

Yet we must remember that He is also on the throne of grace. This grace is intended not only for those being persecuted but also for their persecutors.

If postponement of justice for one more day results in bringing one more person into the Kingdom of Christ, then so be it. Remember, for the Lord a thousand years is like a single day.

If a million years from now we were to ask ourselves whether our momentary suffering during our earthly life was an acceptable change for one more soul to enter into eternal glory, how would we answer?

When considering these hard, but wonderful truths, I am reminded of the Roman centurion who was in charge of the crucifixion of Christ. Listen to him:

When the centurion and those who were with him, keeping watch over Jesus, saw the earthquake and what took place, they were filled with awe and said, *"Truly this was the Son of God!"* (Matthew 27:54).

I wouldn't be surprised if this Roman centurion and some of his men, who led the military unit assigned to crucify our Lord, will reign with us in glory. (In fact, historic tradition says that they became Christians). Such is the long-suffering of Him who sits on the throne of grace.

Warriors, consider this: Being imprisoned is not so bad, for prisoners are not as distracted as those on the outside and therefore the message of the gospel can be more powerful in a prison environment.

They do not put hope in their plans for worldly success, and they think about the end of life more than those on the outside.

Tell them about Jesus, and they are much more eager to hear. "If the Son sets you free, you are free indeed." That is real freedom.

One man stands inside a prison and is free. Another man stands outside a prison in luxurious living and is in bondage.

My brothers and sisters in Christ, also remember this well: we are alive this day because Jesus has a mission for us yet to be fulfilled.

When we die, that will be a sign that He wishes us to do something else.

Eternal missions await each of us. We must move forward in our assignments each and every day of our short lives in this world.

Our deepest motivation must be to hear Him tell us face to face…

......*'Well done, good and faithful servant. You have been faithful over a little; I will set you over much. Enter into the joy of your master"* (Matthew 25:21).

> **"Christian warriors, we are called to fight, not run from the battle!"**

Additional Resources

The most important resource for growing up into the true Christ is the Bible. Chose a translation that is word for word, stay away from the thought for thought translations, and chose one that you can easily read such as the English Standard Version.

Concentrate on understanding what Jesus taught (all that he taught). Avoid what I call designer Bibles, where prominent leaders add their footnotes and interpretations that all too often skew or slant scripture towards their faulty doctrines.

Use a dictionary to look up the meaning of words that you might not be familiar with, and study while asking the Holy Spirit to illuminate the true meaning of those passages and the words of Christ that seem difficult to understand.

The following titles are recommended to help you progress with you walk with Christ. The key is work with the Lord in his discipline, grow in His grace, and be filled with His fullness.

**God's Anointed Warriors
By Dr. Donald Bell**

(available now.)

This book brings 21st century clarity to prophetic events recorded in the book of Revelation and the Lord's calling for warrior-spirited Christians of this generation.

We are right on the verge of devastating events that will create great fear and chaos throughout the world and especially in our increasingly immoral and comfort-seeking nation.

The reader is encouraged to follow Dr. Donald Bell in his in-depth study of Scripture that will bring greater clarity to numerous end-time events recorded in the Book of Revelation -events which are currently unfolding before our very eyes.

For speaking engagements:
DonBell@wvpbooks.com ~ (888) 575-9626 Ext. 780
Dr. Bell's website: www.equippingwatchmen.com

ISBN 978-1-943412-08-2

Published by -
Wilderness Voice Publishing
Canon City, Colorado USA
www.wvpbooks.com

You can obtain this resource by the following:
- Amazon.com - Search: God's Anointed Warriors By Dr. Donald Bell
- Order from your local bookstore: ISBN 978-1-943412-08-2

The Horsemen Cometh
3rd Edition:
Racing Towards the Midnight Cry
By Charles Pretlow

Christian, it is time to wake up! It is time to embrace the truth and break the spell of false teachings and myths about the end of this age. Christ's words are coming to pass rapidly, and few are ready to serve in His power and protection.

The Horsemen Cometh – 3rd edition: Racing Towards the Midnight Cry is an astonishing work that confronts the spell over God's people. With Biblical truth—the author addresses how to become ready—God's way!

These 2004 warnings in this volume are left as first written and are coming to pass rapidly. America is at war with terrorism, Russia and China are rattling their sabers, and Christians are being driven into the closet. Few agreed back in 2004 when these warnings were first given, but see the accuracy of just a few headline warnings when this prophetic warning was first published in 2004:

GOD WILL NO LONGER HOLD BACK THE TIDE of perversion. NUCLEAR WEAPONS OF MASS DESTRUCTION RESURRECTED CHRISTIAN-BASHING WILL BE THE "IN THING TO DO"

For speaking engagements:
Pastor Charles Pretlow ~ PO Box 400, Canon City, CO 81215
www.cpretlow.com ~ chuck@cpretlow.com
(888) 575-9626 Ext. 725
ISBN 978-1-943412-04-4

Published by -
Wilderness Voice Publishing
Canon City, Colorado USA
www.wvpbooks.com **You can obtain this resource by the following:**

- Amazon.com - Search: The Horsemen Cometh By Charles Pretlow
- Order from your local bookstore: ISBN 978-1-943412-04-4

**Midnight Cry Awakening
by Charles Pretlow**
Available in fall of 2018
Most Christians are walking in their sleep concerning the important things of God that facilitate clear thinking, purity, spiritual strength, and discernment. Few are able to endure the coming dark hour. Scripture refers to the close of this age as having troubling birth pangs, global persecution, and a final period called the Great Tribulation.

This volume presents Christ's version concerning the sequencing of the events leading to the end-of-this-age. Our message is for the sincere believer who prefers truth over myth and sound doctrine over faulty theology—this message is for the Christian who desires to wake up and become ready before the midnight cry awakening—and be used by God on the day that he acts. **Coming in the fall of 2018.**

www.ingramcontent.com/pod-product-compliance
Lightning Source LLC
Chambersburg PA
CBHW020024050426
42450CB00005B/640